初岸
true
land

与
美
同
栖

［英］T.S. 艾略特－著

雷格－译

姜瑾－绘

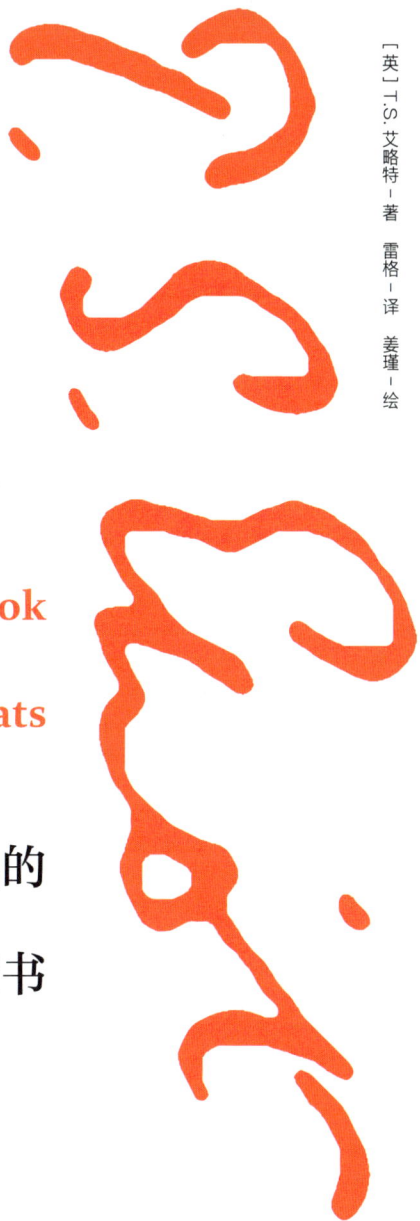

# Old Possum's Book

# of Practical Cats

# 老负鼠的

# 现世猫书

国际文化出版公司

·北京·

# Contents

Preface·······················XXI

The Naming of Cats································002

The Old Gumbie Cat·······························008

Growltiger's Last Stand···························016

The Rum Tum Tugger····························026

The Song of the Jellicles·························034

Mungojerrie and Rumpelteazer·················042

Old Deuteronomy································050

Of the Aweful Battle of the Pekes and the Pollicles···058

Mr. Mistoffelees································068

Macavity: The Mystery Cat····················078

Gus: The Theatre Cat···························086

Bustopher Jones: The Cat about Town···············096

Skimbleshanks: The Railway Cat··················104

The Ad-dressing of Cats························114

Cat Morgan Introduces Himself·····················124

# 目 录

以猫为名，给爱猫人士的情书 ································ IV

一幅猫画就是一部猫生电影 ······························ XVI

前言 ·································································· XXI


为猫命名 ····························································004

老甘比猫 ····························································011

咕噜虎的最后一战 ···············································020

吐司酱涂哥 ·························································029

小可爱猫之歌 ······················································037

呢绒夜壶和皱纹诱惑 ············································045

老申命 ·······························································053

狮子狗与小破狗恶斗记 ·········································062

迷思托菲利斯先生 ···············································072

麦卡维蒂：神秘猫 ···············································081

嘎斯：剧院猫 ······················································090

巴士托弗·琼斯：城市游荡猫 ································099

废话脚杆：铁路猫 ···············································108

猫的称呼 ····························································118

摩根猫自我介绍 ···················································126

以猫为名，

给爱猫人士的情书

雷　格

2020 年 5 月 13 日 于北京

## 诗歌大师的另一面

《老负鼠的现世猫书》是英国大诗人 T.S.艾略特 1939 年出版的一本儿童诗集。

艾略特作为现代派诗歌大师，一向善于驾驭宏大主题，比如用《荒原》揭示西方现代社会的精神危机，用《四个四重奏》对时间进行形而上的终极思索；他的个人风格也是如此，严肃得近乎刻板，温文尔雅而又拒人千里，像弗吉尼亚·伍尔夫所嘲笑的那样，常年穿着他的四件套西装，而且因为"一成不变的庄重"被人取了个绰号叫"殡葬师"。

但是这本《老负鼠的现世猫书》，却让我们看到了大师的另一面：诙谐、可爱、刁钻，又充满温情。

这些猫诗纯属游戏之作，最初都出现在艾略特同友人的通信中，本来是他为两个教子写的，其中的一个就是他所在费伯出版社的老板杰弗里·费伯的小孙子托马斯·费伯。诗集初版时收录了 14 首诗，1952 年再版时又增加了一首《摩根猫自我介绍》，这样一共是 15 首。

书名中的"老负鼠"，是美国诗人埃兹拉·庞德给老朋友艾略特取的绰号。当时，他们两位都特别喜欢乔尔·哈里斯编辑整理的童话《雷默斯大叔》，就用其中的角色"负鼠先生""兔子先生"互相称呼，于是艾略特就成了"老负鼠"。这个名字放在他身上还是蛮贴切的，因为他就像负鼠一样爱装死、爱扮惨，把一颗童心掩藏在不苟言笑的外表下。艾略特也很喜欢这个绰号，给朋友写信时就往往落款"老负鼠"，或者是缩写"O.P."。

从这本诗集首次出版到现在，已经 80 多年了。80 多年来，这些妙趣横生的小诗给孩子们，也给无数爱猫人士带来了无尽的欢乐。

### 给你的猫取个酷酷的名字

一个人养猫，最重要的事情是什么？喂食、铲屎、爱抚、逗它玩？这都不够。艾略特煞有介事地正告我们，养猫头等大事乃是为猫取名字：

你乍一听会觉得我是发了疯

　要是我跟你说，一只猫必须有三个不一样

的名字。

——《为猫命名》


　　正所谓"名不正则言不顺"。作为一个资深猫奴，艾略特本人就热衷于给自己的一众爱猫取名字，也会应朋友和陌生人的请托，为他们的猫取名字。

　　这些名字往往脑洞大开、出人意表、欢乐无比。有的我们能明白是什么意思，比如，Pettipaws 意思是"小爪子"，Sillabub 意思是"牛奶葡萄酒"；有的我们知道是他在卖弄学识，比如，George Pushdragon 指的是基督教传说中的屠龙英雄圣乔治，Tumble Brutus 影射古罗马时候组织刺杀恺撒的元老院议员布鲁图；有的就只能猜个大概了，比如，Jellylorum 是说猫的脑门像果冻一样软，Wiscus 是说猫的胡子有特点，Mungojerrie 和 Rumpelteaze 则是把两个不相干的词搞笑地组合在一起，我暂且译成"呢绒夜壶"和"皱纹诱惑"。

艾略特把这些猫大都写到了诗里。比如《猫的称呼》里写道：

我认识一只猫，他有个习惯，

只吃兔肉，别的一星儿都不沾，

吃完以后还要舔爪子，

以免浪费了洋葱汁。

这里说的就是"小爪子"。而"呢绒夜壶"和"皱纹诱惑"，在诗里变成了一对喜欢恶作剧、结伴行窃的贼猫。

教子托马斯·费伯过四岁生日时，艾略特为他写下了这样的妙语：

恭请所有小破狗和小可爱猫莅临托马斯·费伯的生日会。

"小破狗"就是 Pollicle dog，"小可爱猫"就是 Jellicle cat，都是小托马斯的发明；他本来想说的是"poor little dog"（"可怜的小狗"）和"dear little cat"（"亲爱的小猫"），可是小孩子口齿不清、发音不准，结果就成了这个样子。艾略特也把它们写进了《小可爱猫之歌》和《狮子狗与小破狗恶斗记》，让它们在他的诗里得以永生。

向艾略特先生学习，也给你的爱猫取个酷酷的名字吧，取一个比花花、小黑和小黄更特别、更有创意的名字。

## 写猫就是写人生

猫有了名字，也就有了性格。

艾略特在《老负鼠的现世猫书》里写到了各式各样、各种性格的猫，堪称猫类大全。如果换一个角度看，他所写的分明就是人性，就是人生百态，只不过用滑稽、戏谑的拟人化方式展现出来而已。

这里面有德高望重的长寿老猫老申命，有好汉专提当年勇的过气明星、"剧院猫"嘎斯，有时尚先锋、"贪吃猫"巴士托弗·琼斯，有犯罪大师、"神秘猫"麦卡维蒂，有技艺高超的"魔法猫"迷思托菲利斯，有劳动模范、"铁路猫"废话脚杆，有爱操心的"保姆猫"珍妮点点，也有儿女情长紧接着英雄末路的"黑帮猫"咕噜虎。

当艾略特让这些有人性的猫在 20 世纪二三十年代伦敦的各个花园、广场、街区中出没、活动，这些猫诗又赋有了另外的功能：为当时的英国社会生活与城市风情作漫像式的侧写。

比如，衣着讲究、喜欢美食的大胖猫巴士托弗·琼斯所在的圣詹姆士街和蓓尔美尔街，不止在那个年代热闹非凡，即便在今天也是伦敦城的商业中心；诗里提到的好多俱乐部、会所和高档餐厅，估计名字都还在。又如，《摩根猫自我介绍》中提到的布鲁姆斯伯里地区，是伦敦城的文化中心，文化人、艺术家扎堆，学术、教育、出版机构扎堆。当时，这里最有名的精英群体叫"布鲁姆斯伯里文化圈"，以小说家弗吉尼亚·伍尔夫为首，其他大咖还有哲学家罗素、经济学家凯恩斯、小说家 E.M. 福斯特等，艾略特应该算是咖位比较小的新人。直到今天，这里仍是全球文艺青年朝圣的目的地。

话又说回来，艾略特笔下的猫就算再像人，也从未丧失过猫的本来特征。

比如，《吐司酱涂哥》里那只猫，我行我素，拒不合作，逆反，让人读来恨得牙痒痒：

吐司酱涂哥是个无聊透顶的家伙：

你放他进屋里，他却要留在外头；

他总在一扇门错误的一侧，

刚回了家，他又想出去走走。

艾略特在这里并没有一丁点夸张，他把握得极为精准到位。

我家有只猫名叫"剩余价值"。我工作时为了保持安静，会把书房的门关上。这时本来一直趴着打盹的"剩余价值"一准会在外面哀号、抓门，闹着要进来。开门放它进来，它又没有什么正经事找我，转了一圈后又闹着出去——它只是不想让门关着。你看，猫就是这副德行，跟艾略特描写的一模一样！

### 艾略特的诗和音乐剧《猫》

可能有的朋友知道，风靡全球的经典音乐剧《猫》，就是英国作曲家安德鲁·劳埃德·韦伯根据艾略特的《老负鼠的现世猫书》改编的。这部剧于 1981 年 5 月 11

日首演，是史上最卖座的音乐剧之一。

问题是，看过这部剧的人会发现，剧中最光彩夺目的角色、那只最终获得升天资格的"魅力猫"格里莎贝拉，在艾略特这部诗集中根本找不到，那个著名唱段《回忆》也找不到。

这是怎么回事？答案还要从艾略特本人身上找。

韦伯也是个资深猫奴，还是艾略特的粉丝，熟读《老负鼠的现世猫书》，一直想把它搬上舞台，但是苦于找不到好的呈现方式；直到有一次，艾略特的遗孀瓦莱丽给了他一份打字稿。那是一首只有短短八行的小诗：


她多次出没于一个低俗的度假村，

就在肮脏的托特纳姆宫路附近；

她在"无人地带"穿梭奔走，

从"旭日东升"直到"身边好友"。

邮差挠挠头，叹了口气：

"你以为她应该早就死去，

可是谁又能够想到

那就是格里莎贝拉，魅力猫！"

这就是"魅力猫"的原型。不过艾略特觉得"魅力猫"的故事太过悲伤，不适合给孩子们看，就没有收到诗集里。

但是韦伯找到了灵感的突破口。他把格里莎贝拉设计成音乐剧的灵魂人物，以她为核心设计情节，还从艾略特的另一首诗《大风夜狂想曲》中选取了一段文字，谱曲成为《回忆》，让格里莎贝拉在舞台上深情地唱出。事实证明，这首打动人心的歌成为《猫》成功的关键。

## 谐趣诗也要写出大师范儿

事实上，不讲求意义和教谕，唯以幽默、欢乐、韵律是虑的诗，正是英国诗歌中的一个悠久传统，很多诗就是为幼儿做语言训练、审美启蒙用的。其中最著名的是爱德华·李尔的"废话诗"和刘易斯·卡罗尔的"打油诗"。艾略特的谐趣猫诗，可以说是和他们一脉相承的。

不过，谐趣归谐趣，《老负鼠的现世猫书》仍然展现出艾略特作为诗歌大师的非凡功力。除去在施展想象力等方面的超卓表现，他在诗歌形式和技巧上也极为用心。

　　咱们就单说说他的押韵吧。除了常见的联韵（AABB）、交韵（ABAB）、偶韵（ABCB）和抱韵（ABBA）等韵式，他还会选择更为复杂的韵式，比如行内韵与偶韵的结合，就像这样：



所以，就用这种方式，巴士托弗打发着日子——

在这家或那家俱乐部现身。

没什么好惊讶，就在我们眼皮底下

他明显变得圆滚滚。

　　　　　　　——《巴士托弗·琼斯：城市游荡猫》



还有这样：



他沿着过道溜达，仔细检查

头等车和三等车所有旅客的面孔；

他的巡逻很有规律，建立了控制体系；

他马上就会知道有什么事情发生。

　　　　　　　——《废话脚杆：铁路猫》

艾略特这样做可不仅仅是炫技。读起来音韵铿锵、琅琅上口，给读者愉悦、欢快的视听享受，本来就是谐趣诗题中应有之义；内容可以无稽，形式上可马虎不得。所以翻译时我没敢用散文体处理它们，而是尽量依照原来的韵式译出，敬请朋友们参详。

据瓦莱丽回忆，艾略特本人对自己这本小书也相当珍爱，常常拿一本放在床头，还不时改动诗句中的一两个字，念念有词。我听到过艾略特自己诵读这 15 首猫诗的音频，算是他自己对这些诗的阐发，有趣得紧。朋友们如有兴趣，可以找来听听。

再配上姜瑾博士凭借她的个性化理解、以独创的彩墨晕染技法精心绘就的猫画，一道爱猫大餐就这么成了。希望你喜欢。

一幅猫画

就是一部猫生电影

姜　瑾

2020 年 2 月 于瑞典

# Happiness is to be owned by a cat！

（幸福就是当上猫奴！）

一辆湖蓝色的老式甲壳虫车，在冬日灰蒙蒙的斯德哥尔摩大街上格外抢眼，车身上用酒红色的字写着这句话。我想所有爱猫之人看到了，都会像我一样心领神会，莞尔一笑，你懂的。我养猫 30 余年，爱猫如子，所以当雷格先生邀请我为此书作插画时，便心生欢喜，欣然应允了。

根据编辑的提议，我在这里简单叙述一下这 15 幅画的创作过程。

## 构思：读懂诗人（understand the story）

T.S. 艾略特这 15 首著名的猫诗，巧妙地把猫的那些伶俐的小德性与人类的生活百态糅在了一起，勾画出 15 个"猫生"，每只猫都是一个"人物"，所以，为这些诗作插画就像为 15 部电影做海报。

诗要慢读，好比精酿的老酒需要慢慢品出里面的层次，每一句都是浓缩的精华。静下来，一遍遍读出诗里诗外、诗前诗后的意思，才能读懂诗人的心；懂了，就可以在脑子里看小电影了。以诗为剧本，我先为故事选好了演员，再设计出故事发生的时间、地点、场景和道具，让小电影先在脑子里演几遍，然后定格一个最生动的画面，构思便完成了。

### 造型：它是谁（know the character）

艾略特的这些猫个性分明，千伶百俐，每个故事都是掷地有声的，主角的"猫生"造就了它的气质，以及它眼睛里的光。猫固然只只可爱，但绝不是小清新的风格，即便是最大的坏蛋，也是猫性十足，诙谐而有范儿。猫生来优雅，但绝不柔弱，所以，画的时候特地选用了敦厚的欧洲古法制作的彩墨，色彩饱和度高，对比度比较强，在造型与轮廓上也注重比较厚实的感觉。

# 场景：抓住诗的情绪（capture the mood）

　　艾略特的这些猫诗，拥有世界上所有的空间与时间，所以每幅画都可以在任何年代与地点取景，这样大的想象空间，画起来自然就很有趣了。我想，每幅画都要美，要有光，要有一种特殊的气氛，这个气氛取决于这首诗所表达的情绪。在构思的时候，我着重于解析每个故事的情绪，是快乐、忧伤、神秘、孤独，诙谐，还是甜美；以及这个情绪的温度，是暖色调，还是冷色调。然后，把这种情绪通过画的气氛和色彩表达出来。比如以下这些场景的选择：在北欧冬日的荒原上，缥缈的极光下，有驶向远山的火车；在英伦的岛屿上，宁静的夏日午后，有艾略特的写字台；在午夜的湖边，静谧的水草丛中，有隐身的夜行者；在美洲的荒原上，正午的骄阳下，有充满杀机的老街；在远山夕阳下，有森林里的动物小剧场；还有月光下开满夜来香与昙花的秘密花园。如此种种，都是对诗的演绎式的阐释。

## 技法：工匠的享受（the artisan's pleasure）

　　构图和造型的出发点是想把每幅画当成一幅绘画作品去画，并没有局限在插图的理念中。在这个插图已经数码化的时代，我此次还是选择了完全的手工绘画，每幅从构思到完成需要至少一周的时间。彩墨一层层地晕染上去，有种工匠式的享受，同时可以收获手工绘画时材料出现的意外效果。画得慢，画得开心，也希望读者看得慢看得开心。同时，我相信每位细心的读者，读了这些诗以后，心中都有一部属于自己的小电影。

# Preface　　前 言

This book is respectfully dedicated to those friends who have assisted its composition by their encouragement, criticism and suggestions: and in particular to Mr. T. E. Faber, Miss Alison Tandy, Miss Susan Wolcott, Miss Susanna Morley, and the Man in White Spats.

O. P.

谨以此书敬献那些提出鼓励、批评和建议以襄其成的朋友，并特别敬献 T. E. 费伯先生、艾丽森·坦迪小姐、苏珊·沃尔科特小姐、苏珊娜·莫利小姐，以及穿白鞋套的男人。

老负鼠

# The

# Naming

# of

# Cats

The Naming of Cats is a difficult matter,

    It isn't just one of your holiday games;

You may think at first I'm as mad as a hatter

    When I tell you, a cat must have THREE DIFFERENT NAMES.

First of all, there's the name that the family use daily,

    Such as Peter, Augustus, Alonzo or James,

Such as Victor or Jonathan, George or Bill Bailey—

    All of them sensible everyday names.

There are fancier names if you think they sound sweeter,

    Some for the gentlemen, some for the dames:

Such as Plato, Admetus, Electra, Demeter—

    But all of them sensible everyday names.

But I tell you, a cat needs a name that's particular,

    A name that's peculiar, and more dignified,

Else how can he keep up his tail perpendicular,

    Or spread out his whiskers, or cherish his pride?

Of names of this kind, I can give you a quorum,

    Such as Munkustrap, Quaxo, or Coricopat,

Such as Bombalurina, or else Jellylorum—

    Names that never belong to more than one cat.

But above and beyond there's still one name left over,

    And that is the name that you never will guess;

The name that no human research can discover—

    But THE CAT HIMSELF KNOWS, and will never confess.

When you notice a cat in profound meditation,

    The reason, I tell you, is always the same:

His mind is engaged in a rapt contemplation

    Of the thought, of the thought, of the thought of his name:

        His ineffable effable

        Effanineffable

Deep and inscrutable singular Name.

# 为猫命名

为猫命名是件困难事情，

　　那可不像你假日里玩个游戏；

你乍一听会觉得我是发了疯

　　要是我跟你说，一只猫必须有三个不一样的名字。

首先，得有个家里人日常用的名字，

　　比如彼得、奥古斯都、阿隆索或是詹姆斯，

比如维克多或是乔纳森，乔治或是比尔·贝利——

　　全都是入情入理的平常名字。

还有些更炫酷的名字，如果你想让它们更悦耳，

　　有的适合先生，有的适合女士：

比如柏拉图、阿德墨托斯、厄勒克特拉、德墨忒耳——

　　但这全都是入情入理的平常名字。

可我告诉你，一只猫需要一个特别的名字，

　　这名字要不同凡响，更加富丽堂皇，

否则他凭什么把尾巴翘得笔直，

　　或是乍开胡须，或是得意扬扬？

说到这类名字，我能给你举出一组，

　　比如蒙库斯陷阱、夸克索或是科里科拍打，

比如炸弹鲁丽娜，要么就用果冻洛卢姆——

　　这类专属名号绝不会有第二只猫领下。

但是还剩下一个无与伦比的名字，

　　这个名字你绝对猜不出来；

人类的所有研究都不能将它揭示——

　　但是**猫自己知道**，而永远不会坦白。

当你注意到一只猫陷入玄想，

　　个中原因，我告诉你，总是一致：

他的头脑正专注于苦思冥想

　　他的名字的奥义、奥义、奥义：

　　　　他那不可言说而可言说的

　　　　可言说而不可言说的

高深、难解、独一无二的名字。

# The

# Old

# Gumbie

# Cat

I have a Gumbie Cat in mind, her name is Jennyanydots;

Her coat is of the tabby kind, with tiger stripes and leopard spots.

All day she sits upon the stair or on the steps or on the mat:

She sits and sits and sits and sits—and that's what makes a Gumbie Cat!


But when the day's hustle and bustle is done,

Then the Gumbie Cat's work is but hardly begun.

And when all the family's in bed and asleep,

She slips down the stairs to the basement to creep.

She is deeply concerned with the ways of the mice—

Their behaviour's not good and their manners not nice;

So when she has got them lined up on the matting,

She teaches them music, crocheting and tatting.


I have a Gumbie Cat in mind, her name is Jennyanydots;

Her equal would be hard to find, she likes the warm and sunny spots.

All day she sits beside the hearth or in the sun or on my hat:

She sits and sits and sits and sits—and that's what makes a Gumbie Cat!


But when the day's hustle and bustle is done,

Then the Gumbie Cat's work is but hardly begun.

As she finds that the mice will not ever keep quiet,

She is sure it is due to irregular diet;

And believing that nothing is done without trying,

She sets straight to work with her baking and frying.

She makes them a mouse-cake of bread and dried peas,

And a beautiful fry of lean bacon and cheese.

I have a Gumbie Cat in mind, her name is Jennyanydots;

The curtain-cord she likes to wind, and tie it into sailor-knots.

She sits upon the window-sill, or anything that's smooth and flat:

She sits and sits and sits and sits—and that's what makes a Gumbie Cat!


But when the day's hustle and bustle is done,

Then the Gumbie Cat's work is but hardly begun.

She thinks that the cockroaches just need employment

To prevent them from idle and wanton destroyment.

So she's formed, from that lot of disorderly louts,

A troop of well-disciplined helpful boy-scouts,

With a purpose in life and a good deed to do—

And she's even created a Beetles' Tattoo.


So for Old Gumbie Cats let us now give three cheers—

On whom well-ordered households depend, it appears.

# 老甘比猫

我心中有一只甘比猫,她的名字叫珍妮点点;

她穿着斑猫类型的外套,上面有虎纹和豹斑。

她整天在楼梯上、台阶上或地毯上安坐:

她坐呀坐呀坐呀坐——甘比猫就是那样坐成的!


然而一天的忙碌喧嚣结束之时,

甘比猫的工作才算刚刚开始。

当所有家人都已经上床睡觉,

她溜下楼梯进了地下室蹑手蹑脚。

她深深关切耗子们的处世之道——

他们行为不端,他们举止不好;

所以她让他们在垫子上排成队列,

教他们音乐、钩编和花边梭结。


我心中有一只甘比猫,她的名字叫珍妮点点;

能跟她媲美的猫很难找,她喜欢温暖向阳的地点。

她整天在壁炉前、阳光下或是我的帽子上安坐:

她坐呀坐呀坐呀坐——甘比猫就是那样坐成的!

然而一天的忙碌喧嚣结束之时，

甘比猫的工作才算刚刚开始。

她发现耗子们永远不会保持安静，

就断定这是由饮食不规律造成。

她相信除了尝试别无他法，

就马上动手，又是烤又是炸。

她给他们做了面包和干豌豆的老鼠蛋糕，

还有美味的煎精肉培根配奶酪。


我心中有一只甘比猫，她的名字叫珍妮点点；

她喜欢拿着窗帘绳缠绕，打成水手结一团团。

她在窗台上，或者任何光滑的平面上安坐：

她坐呀坐呀坐呀坐——甘比猫就是那样坐成的！


然而一天的忙碌喧嚣结束之时，

甘比猫的工作才算刚刚开始。

她认为蟑螂们需要就业机会

才能免于无所事事，恣意妄为。

于是她把那群目无法纪的恶棍

编成了一支纪律严明、乐于助人的童子军。

有善事可做，有生活目标——

她甚至创作了一曲甲虫归营鼓号。


就现在，让我们为老甘比猫们欢呼三次——
秩序井然的家庭全靠他们，看来如此。

# Growltiger's

# Last

# Stand

Growltiger was a Bravo Cat, who travelled on a barge:
In fact he was the roughest cat that ever roamed at large.
From Gravesend up to Oxford he pursued his evil aims,
Rejoicing in his title of "The Terror of the Thames".

His manners and appearance did not calculate to please;
His coat was torn and seedy, he was baggy at the knees;
One ear was somewhat missing, no need to tell you why,
And he scowled upon a hostile world from one forbidding eye.

The cottagers of Rotherhithe knew something of his fame;
At Hammersmith and Putney people shuddered at his name.
They would fortify the hen-house, lock up the silly goose,
When the rumour ran along the shore: GROWLTIGER'S ON THE LOOSE!

Woe to the weak canary, that fluttered from its cage;

Woe to the pampered Pekinese, that faced Growltiger's rage;

Woe to the bristly Bandicoot, that lurks on foreign ships,

And woe to any Cat with whom Growltiger came to grips!


But most to Cats of foreign race his hatred had been vowed;

To Cats of foreign name and race no quarter was allowed.

The Persian and the Siamese regarded him with fear—

Because it was a Siamese had mauled his missing ear.


Now on a peaceful summer night, all nature seemed at play,

The tender moon was shining bright, the barge at Molesey lay.

All in the balmy moonlight it lay rocking on the tide—

And Growltiger was disposed to show his sentimental side.

His bucko mate, GRUMBUSKIN, long since had disappeared,

For to the Bell at Hampton he had gone to wet his beard;

And his bosun, TUMBLEBRUTUS, he too had stol'n away—

In the yard behind the Lion he was prowling for his prey.


In the forepeak of the vessel Growltiger sate alone,

Concentrating his attention on the Lady GRIDDLEBONE.

And his raffish crew were sleeping in their barrels and their bunks—

As the Siamese came creeping in their sampans and their junks.


Growltiger had no eye or ear for aught but Griddlebone,

And the Lady seemed enraptured by his manly baritone,

Disposed to relaxation, and awaiting no surprise—

But the moonlight shone reflected from a hundred bright blue eyes.


And closer still and closer the sampans circled round,

And yet from all the enemy there was not heard a sound.

The lovers sang their last duet, in danger of their lives—

For the foe was armed with toasting forks and cruel carving knives.


Then GILBERT gave the signal to his fierce Mongolian horde;

With a frightful burst of fireworks the Chinks they swarmed aboard.

Abandoning their sampans, and their pullaways and junks,

They battened down the hatches on the crew within their bunks.


Then Griddlebone she gave a screech, for she was badly skeered;

I am sorry to admit it, but she quickly disappeared.

She probably escaped with ease, I'm sure she was not drowned—

But a serried ring of flashing steel Growltiger did surround.

The ruthless foe pressed forward, in stubborn rank on rank;

Growltiger to his vast surprise was forced to walk the plank.

He who a hundred victims had driven to that drop,

At the end of all his crimes was forced to go ker-flip, ker-flop.

Oh there was joy in Wapping when the news flew through the land;

At Maidenhead and Henley there was dancing on the strand.

Rats were roasted whole at Brentford, and at Victoria Dock,

And a day of celebration was commanded in Bangkok.

# 咕噜虎的最后一战

**咕噜虎**是一只亡命猫，他航行在一条驳船上面；

实际上他是史上最强横的猫，一直没有归案。

从格雷夫森德到牛津，他追逐着他的罪恶目标，

因此拥有了"泰晤士河恐怖"的名号。


他的举止和仪表从不讨人喜爱；

他的外套又脏又破，他有着松垮垮的膝盖；

一只耳朵不见了，没必要告诉你因为什么，

他用冷酷的独眼怒对这充满敌意的世界。


罗瑟希德的村民多少知道他的名头；

在哈默史密斯和普特尼，人们提起他的威名就发抖。

他们会加固鸡舍，把呆鹅关牢，

因为有流言沿着河岸传来：**咕噜虎越狱在逃！**


柔弱的金丝雀有祸了，他从笼子里飞出；

受宠的狮子狗有祸了，他要面对咕噜虎的暴怒。

生硬毛的袋狸有祸了，他在外国轮船上潜伏，

所有的猫有祸了，假如他们被咕噜虎揪住！


不过外国种的猫最让他起誓痛恨；

对外国名和外国种的猫他格杀勿论。

波斯猫和暹罗猫提起他就大惊失色——

因为就是一只暹罗猫咬掉了他的一只耳朵。


在这样一个安宁的夏夜，万物似乎都在游戏，

月色柔和明亮，驳船停靠在莫莱西。

温暖的月光下，潮水上摇荡着驳船——

咕噜虎有意展示他多愁善感的一面。


他的恶棍大副，**牢骚皮**，已经消失很久，

他去了汉普顿的大钟酒吧喝酒；

偷偷溜走的还有水手长，**打滚布鲁图**——

在雄狮酒吧后院，他游来荡去搜寻猎物。


咕噜虎独自坐在船艄舱，

心思全在**烤盘骨头**女士身上。

他那些散漫的船员正在桶里铺上睡觉——

这时暹罗猫们驾着舢板和帆船悄悄来到。


咕噜虎的眼里耳中除了烤盘骨头别无他物，

这位女士似乎也被他那雄性的男中音迷住，

不自觉放松了，没想到意外发生——

但是反射月光的，是一百只明亮的蓝眼睛。


舢板兜着圈子围得越来越近，

然而敌方阵营里听不到一点声音。

生命危险中，两个恋人唱着他们最后一曲二重唱——

因为对手已经用烤叉和残忍的切肉刀将自己武装。


然后**吉尔伯特**向他凶残的蒙古部落发出信号；

他们蜂拥而上，将可怕的中国烟花燃爆。

他们抛开舢板，抛开拖船和帆船，

封死了舱门，将船员们困在铺位里面。


然后烤盘骨头发出一声尖叫，因为她给吓得不轻；

我很不情愿承认，但她迅速消失了踪影。

她可能轻易逃脱了，我肯定她没有溺亡——

咕噜虎却被一圈闪亮的钢刃密麻麻围上。


冷酷无情的敌人步步紧逼，严格保持队形相连；

咕噜虎大吃一惊，他要被迫去走船舷外的跳板。

他曾经那样强迫一百个受害者落入水中，

到头来他的累累罪行也终结于扑通一声。


哦，当消息传到沃平，那里一片欢笑；

在梅登黑德和亨利，河滩上跳起了舞蹈。

在布伦特福德和维多利亚码头，吃起了烤全鼠，

在曼谷，用了一整天时间庆祝。

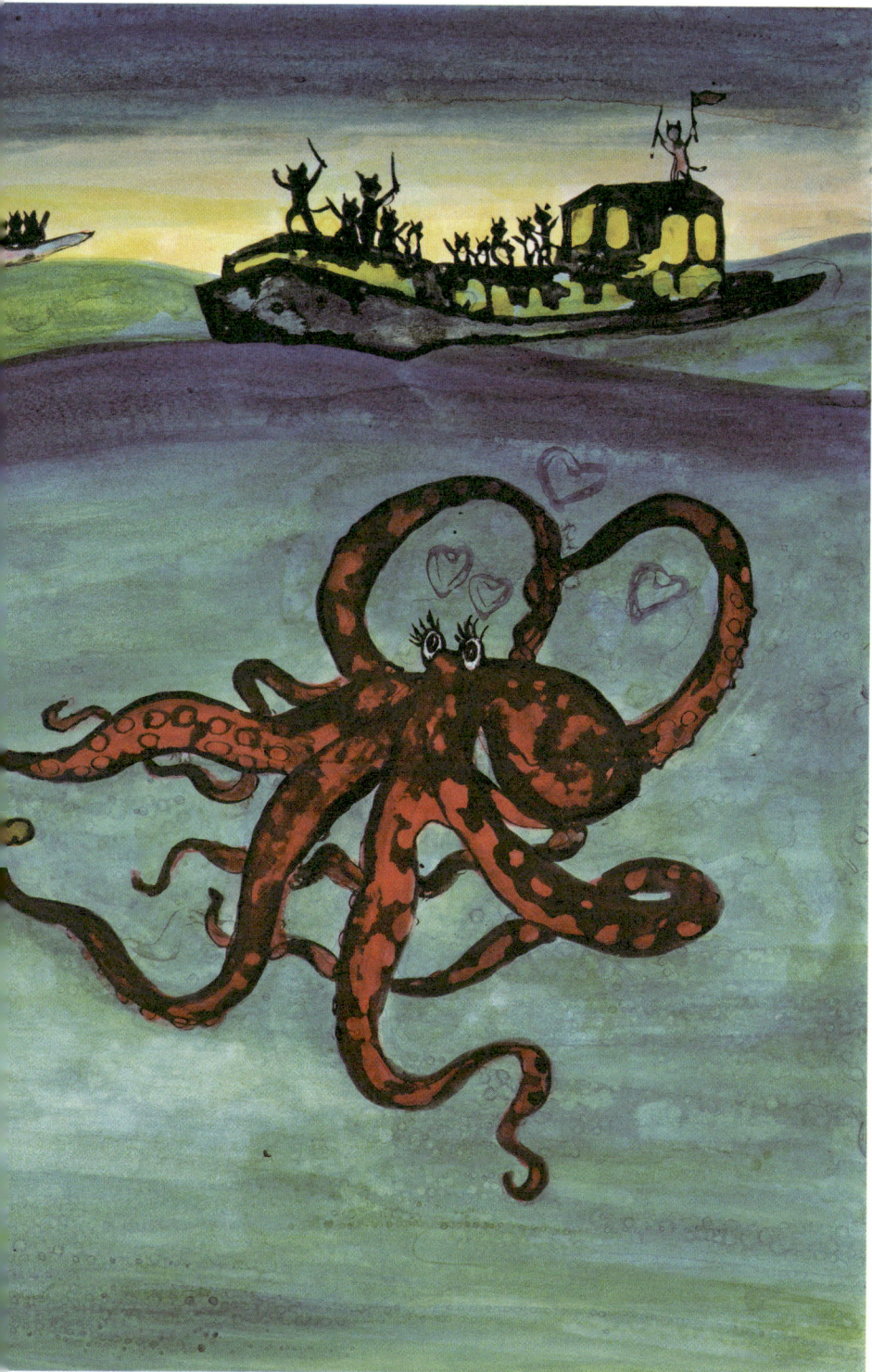

# The
# Rum
# Tum
# Tugger

The Rum Tum Tugger is a Curious Cat:

If you offer him pheasant he would rather have grouse.

If you put him in a house he would much prefer a flat,

If you put him in a flat then he'd rather have a house.

If you set him on a mouse then he only wants a rat,

If you set him on a rat then he'd rather chase a mouse.

Yes the Rum Tum Tugger is a Curious Cat—

    And there isn't any call for me to shout it:

      For he will do

      As he do do

        And there's no doing anything about it!


The Rum Tum Tugger is a terrible bore:

When you let him in, then he wants to be out;

He's always on the wrong side of every door,

And as soon as he's at home, then he'd like to get about.

He likes to lie in the bureau drawer,

But he makes such a fuss if he can't get out.

Yes the Rum Tum Tugger is a Curious Cat—

    And there isn't any use for you to doubt it:

      For he will do

      As he do do

        And there's no doing anything about it!


The Rum Tum Tugger is a curious beast:

His disobliging ways are a matter of habit.

If you offer him fish then he always wants a feast;

When there isn't any fish then he won't eat rabbit.

If you offer him cream then he sniffs and sneers,

For he only likes what he finds for himself;

So you'll catch him in it right up to the ears,

If you put it away on the larder shelf.

The Rum Tum Tugger is artful and knowing,

The Rum Tum Tugger doesn't care for a cuddle;

But he'll leap on your lap in the middle of your sewing,

For there's nothing he enjoys like a horrible muddle.

Yes the Rum Tum Tugger is a Curious Cat—

    And there isn't any need for me to spout it:

        For he will do

        As he do do

            And there's no doing anything about it!

# 吐司酱涂哥

吐司酱涂哥是只古怪猫咪：

你若是喂他野鸡，他倒宁可吃松鸡。

你若是让他住宅子，他却选择公寓，

你若是让他住公寓，他又宁愿住宅子。

你若是让他捉耗子，他却只对大老鼠在意，

你若是让他捉老鼠，他又宁肯去追小耗子。

是的，吐司酱涂哥是只古怪猫——

  而并没有谁要求我高声呼叫：

    因为他想怎样

    就怎样

      对此什么事都做不了！


吐司酱涂哥是个无聊透顶的家伙：

你放他进屋里，他却要留在外头；

他总在一扇门错误的一侧，

刚回了家，他又想出去走走。

他喜欢往办公室的抽屉里一卧，

可是不能出门他又闹个不休。

是的，吐司酱涂哥是只古怪猫——

　　而你去质疑这个也是徒劳：

　　　　因为他想怎样

　　　　就怎样

　　　　　对此什么事都做不了！


吐司酱涂哥是个古怪的混蛋：

他拒不合作的行为方式是个习惯问题。

你若是喂他鱼，他总想着吃大餐；

若是没有鱼，他又不吃兔子。

你若是给他奶油，他就嗤之以鼻，

因为他只喜欢自己找到的东西；

所以你若是把奶油拿开，放上食品柜架子，

准会逮到他在那儿埋头狂吃。

吐司酱涂哥做事狡诈又成心，

吐司酱涂哥对拥抱并不在乎；

但他会跳上你膝头，恰好你在缝纫，

因为他就喜欢把局面搅得一塌糊涂。

是的，吐司酱涂哥是只古怪猫——

　　而我完全没有必要絮絮叨叨：

　　　　因为他想怎样

就怎样

　　对此什么事都做不了!

# The
# Song
#  of
# the
# Jellicles

*Jellicle Cats come out to-night,*
*Jellicle Cats come one come all:*
*The Jellicle Moon is shining bright—*
*Jellicles come to the Jellicle Ball.*


Jellicle Cats are black and white,
Jellicle Cats are rather small;
Jellicle Cats are merry and bright,
And pleasant to hear when they caterwaul.
Jellicle Cats have cheerful faces,
Jellicle Cats have bright black eyes;
They like to practise their airs and graces
And wait for the Jellicle Moon to rise.

Jellicle Cats develop slowly,
Jellicle Cats are not too big;
Jellicle Cats are roly-poly,
They know how to dance a gavotte and a jig.
Until the Jellicle Moon appears
They make their toilette and take their repose:
Jellicles wash behind their ears,
Jellicles dry between their toes.

Jellicle Cats are white and black,
Jellicle Cats are of moderate size;
Jellicles jump like a jumping-jack,

Jellicle Cats have moonlit eyes.

They're quiet enough in the morning hours,

They're quiet enough in the afternoon,

Reserving their terpsichorean powers

To dance by the light of the Jellicle Moon.


Jellicle Cats are black and white,

Jellicle Cats (as I said) are small;

If it happens to be a stormy night

They will practise a caper or two in the hall.

If it happens the sun is shining bright

You would say they had nothing to do at all:

They are resting and saving themselves to be right

For the Jellicle Moon and the Jellicle Ball.

# 小可爱猫之歌

小可爱猫今夜出动，

小可爱猫成群结队，

小可爱月亮皎洁光明——

小可爱猫去赴小可爱舞会。

小可爱猫黑白两色，

小可爱猫娇小体型；

小可爱猫聪明快活，

他们叫春的声音也好听。

小可爱猫生着迷人脸庞，

小可爱猫生着明亮的黑眼睛；

他们喜欢装模作样

等着小可爱月亮初升。

小可爱猫长得很慢，

小可爱猫个头不大；

小可爱猫胖胖圆圆，

他们是加沃特舞和吉格舞行家。

在小可爱月亮现身之前

他们一直在梳妆和休整。

小可爱猫洗净耳朵后面，

小可爱猫舔干脚趾缝。


小可爱猫黑白两色，

小可爱猫身材适中；

小可爱猫跳得像蹦跳杰克，

小可爱猫有着月光照亮的眼睛。

他们在早晨十足安静，

他们在下午安静十足，

为他们的舞蹈积蓄体能

好在小可爱月亮下起舞。


小可爱猫黑白两色，

小可爱猫（如我所说）体型娇小；

假如正赶上暴风雨夜，

他们会在大厅里跳上一跳。

假如正赶上阳光明丽

你会说他们无所作为：

他们在休息和节省体力

只为了小可爱月亮和小可爱舞会。

# Mungojerrie

# and

# Rumpelteazer

Mungojerrie and Rumpelteazer were a very notorious couple of cats.

As knockabout clown, quick-change comedians, tight-rope walkers and
acrobats

They had an extensive reputation. They made their home in Victoria Grove—

That was merely their centre of operation, for they were incurably given
to rove.

They were very well known in Cornwall Gardens, in Launceston Place and
in Kensington Square—

They had really a little more reputation than a couple of cats can very
well bear.

 

   If the area window was found ajar

   And the basement looked like a field of war,

   If a tile or two came loose on the roof,

   Which presently ceased to be waterproof,

   If the drawers were pulled out from the bedroom chests,

   And you couldn't find one of your winter vests,

   Or after supper one of the girls

   Suddenly missed her Woolworth pearls:

Then the family would say: "It's that horrible cat!

It was Mungojerrie—or Rumpelteazer!"—And most of the time they left it
at that.

 

Mungojerrie and Rumpelteazer had a very unusual gift of the gab.

They were highly efficient cat-burglars as well, and remarkably smart at
smash-and-grab.

They made their home in Victoria Grove. They had no regular occupation.

They were plausible fellows, and liked to engage a friendly policeman in
conversation.

When the family assembled for Sunday dinner,

With their minds made up that they wouldn't get thinner

On Argentine joint, potatoes and greens,

And the cook would appear from behind the scenes

And say in a voice that was broken with sorrow:

"I'm afraid you must wait and have dinner *tomorrow*!

For the joint has gone from the oven—like that!"

Then the family would say: "It's that horrible cat!

It was Mungojerrie—or Rumpelteazer!"—And most of the time they left

it at that.


Mungojerrie and Rumpelteazer had a wonderful way of working together.

And some of the time you would say it was luck, and some of the time

you would say it was weather.

They would go through the house like a hurricane, and no sober person

could take his oath

Was it Mungojerrie—or Rumpelteazer? or could you have sworn that it

mightn't be both?


And when you heard a dining-room smash

Or up from the pantry there came a loud crash

Or down from the library came a loud *ping*

From a vase which was commonly said to be Ming—

Then the family would say: "Now which was which cat?

It was Mungojerrie! AND Rumpelteazer!"—And there's nothing at all to

be done about that!

# 呢绒夜壶和皱纹诱惑

呢绒夜壶和皱纹诱惑是一对臭名昭著的猫。

就像闹剧小丑、快速换装滑稽演员、走钢丝艺人和杂技活宝，

他们声名远播。他们把家安在维多利亚格罗夫路上——

那只是他们活动的中心点，因为他们无可救药地习惯于流浪。

他们在康沃尔花园、朗塞斯顿广场和肯辛顿广场尽人皆知——

他们获得的名声还真不是一对猫所能担得起。


假如地下室的窗户半敞，

室内看着好像一片战场，

假如屋顶上有一两块瓦片松动，

当下已丧失了防水功能，

假如卧室衣橱被拉开了抽屉，

你找不到你的马甲式冬衣，

或者某个姑娘吃过晚饭

忽然发现她的伍尔沃思珍珠找不见：

然后这家人会说："是那可恶的猫！

是呢绒夜壶——或者皱纹诱惑！"——而他们通常就那样拉倒。

呢绒夜壶和皱纹诱惑天生三寸不烂之舌。

他们也是技艺高超的猫贼，特别擅长砸橱窗抢劫。

他们把家安在维多利亚路上。他们没有正当职业。

他们是花言巧语的家伙，喜欢跟一个友善的警察闲扯。


一家人周日聚餐的时候

下定决心不能变得更瘦，

得吃阿根廷烤肉、土豆和绿叶菜，

这时厨子会从后厨走出来，

说话声音悲哀又疲倦：

"我恐怕你们要等到明天才能用晚餐！

因为烤肉已经从烤炉里消失——又是这一套！"

然后这家人会说："是那可恶的猫！

是呢绒夜壶——或者皱纹诱惑！"——而他们通常就那样拉倒。


呢绒夜壶和皱纹诱惑有一套联手作案的绝妙法子。

有时你会说这是运气，有时你会说是靠天气。

他们会像一阵飓风扫荡房子，没有哪个清醒的人能起誓说

那是呢绒夜壶——还是皱纹诱惑？或者，你敢说不是两个？

当你听见餐厅里哗啦一响

或是上面食物间传出一声哐啷

或是下面书房传出砰的一声

碎了一只据说是明朝烧制的花瓶——

然后这家人会说："这次到底是哪只猫干的?

是呢绒夜壶和皱纹诱惑一道！"——对此根本就无可奈何！

# Old

# Deuteronomy

Old Deuteronomy's lived a long time;

    He's a Cat who has lived many lives in succession.

He was famous in proverb and famous in rhyme

    A long while before Queen Victoria's accession.

Old Deuteronomy's buried nine wives

    And more—I am tempted to say, ninety-nine;

And his numerous progeny prospers and thrives

    And the village is proud of him in his decline.

At the sight of that placid and bland physiognomy,

    When he sits in the sun on the vicarage wall,

    The Oldest Inhabitant croaks: "Well, of all...

Things...Can it be...really!...No!...Yes!...

    Ho! hi!

    Oh, my eye!

My sight may be failing, but I confess

I *believe* it is Old Deuteronomy!"


Old Deuteronomy sits in the street,

    He sits in the High Street on market day;

The bullocks may bellow, the sheep they may bleat,

    But the dogs and the herdsmen will turn them away.

The cars and the lorries run over the kerb,

    And the villagers put up a notice: ROAD CLOSED—

So that nothing untoward may chance to disturb

    Deuteronomy's rest when he feels so disposed

Or when he's engaged in domestic economy:

    And the Oldest Inhabitant croaks: "Well, of all...

Things...Can it be...really!...No!...Yes!...

    Ho! hi!

Oh, my eye!

I'm deaf of an ear now, but yet I can guess

That the cause of the trouble is Old Deuteronomy!"


Old Deuteronomy lies on the floor

Of the Fox and French Horn for his afternoon sleep;

And when the men say: "There's just time for one more,"

Then the landlady from her back parlour will peep

And say: "New then, out you go, by the back door,

For Old Deuteronomy mustn't be woken—

I'll have the police if there's any uproar"—

And out they all shuffle, without a word spoken.

The digestive repose of that feline's gastronomy

Must never be broken, whatever befall:

And the Oldest Inhabitant croaks: "Well, of all.

Things...Can it be...really!...Yes!...No!...

Ho! hi!

Oh, my eye!

My legs may be tottery, I must go slow

And be careful of Old Deuteronomy!"

# 老申命

老申命 [1] 已经活了很久；

　　他是一只连着过了好几辈子的猫。

他在谚语和儿歌中享有名头

　　可远远早于维多利亚女王荣登大宝。

老申命曾经给九个妻子下葬，

　　甚至不止——我想说的是，有九十九个；

他有子孙无数，蕃盛兴旺，

　　村人都以他为荣，虽然他已日渐衰弱。

见他一副平静安详、无欲无求的面容，

　　正坐在教区牧师家墙头晒太阳，

最老的村民哑着嗓子说："唉，世事无常……

　　偏偏……怎么会……真的！……不！……是的！……

　　　　嚯！嘻！

　　　　哦，我的乖乖！

我的眼神可能不济事了，可我敢说

我相信那就是老申命！"

---

[1]　老申命（Old Deuteronomy），猫名，取自《圣经·旧约·申命记》。

老申命往大街上坐，

　　　他在赶集的日子坐上了街头；

公牛可能会哞哞，绵羊可能会咩咩，

　　　但狗和牧人会把他们统统赶走。

轿车和卡车从路肩碾过，

　　　村民们便贴出告示：**道路封闭——**

这样就不会横生枝节，不经意间搅扰了

　　　老申命休息，当他感觉如此惬意

或者正在参与料理家政：

　　　最老的村民哑着嗓子说："唉，世事无常……

　　　偏偏……怎么会……真的！……不！……是的！……

　　　　　嚯！嘻！

　　　　　哦，我的乖乖！

我如今有一只耳朵聋了，可我敢说

麻烦事的根源就是老申命！"


老申命躺在狐狸和圆号

　　　酒吧的地板上午睡；

当男人们说："再来一杯，时间正好，"

　　　老板娘会从后厅向外偷窥

并且说："听着，你们给我出去，从后门离开，千万不能把老申命吵醒——

要是惹出乱子，我就叫警察来"——

　　他们就都拖着脚出去，一声没吭。

那位猫科美食家的消食小睡万万不能

　　受到惊扰，哪怕是祸从天降：

最老的村民哑着嗓子说："唉，世事无常……

　　偏偏……怎么会……真的！……是的！……不！……

　　　　嚯！嗜！

　　　　哦，我的乖乖！

我的腿脚可能不利落了，我得慢着点走路，

　　千万别惹到老申命！"

# Of the Aweful

# Battle

# of the Pekes

# and the Pollicles

*Together with Some Account*

*of the Participation*

*of the Pugs and the Poms, and the*

*Intervention of the Great Rumpuscat*

The Pekes and the Pollicles, everyone knows,

Are proud and implacable passionate foes;

It is always the same, wherever one goes.

And the Pugs and the Poms, although most people say

That they do not like fighting, will often display

Every symptom of wanting to join in the fray.

And they

      Bark bark bark bark

      Bark bark BARK BARK

  Until you can hear them all over the Park.


Now on the occasion of which I shall speak

Almost nothing had happened for nearly a week

(And that's a long time for a Pol or a Peke).

The big Police Dog was away from his beat—

I don't know the reason, but most people think

He'd slipped into the Bricklayer's Arms for a drink—

And no one at all was about on the street

When a Peke and a Pollicle happened to meet.

They did not advance, or exactly retreat,

But they glared at each other, and scraped their hind feet,

And they started to

      Bark bark bark bark

      Bark bark BARK BARK

  Until you can hear them all over the Park.


Now the Peke, although people may say what they please,

Is no British Dog, but a Heathen Chinese.

And so all the Pekes, when they heard the uproar,

Some came to the window, some came to the door;

There were surely a dozen, more likely a score.

And together they started to grumble and wheeze

In their huffery-snuffery Heathen Chinese.

But a terrible din is what Pollicles like,

For your Pollicle Dog is a dour Yorkshire tyke,

And his braw Scottish cousins are snappers and biters,

And every dog-jack of them notable fighters;

And so they stepped out, with their pipers in order,

Playing *When the Blue Bonnets Came Over the Border*.

Then the Pugs and the Poms held no longer aloof,

But some from the balcony, some from the roof,

Joined in

To the din

With a

      Bark bark bark bark

      Bark bark BARK BARK

  Until you can hear them all over the Park.


Now when these bold heroes together assembled,

The traffic all stopped, and the Underground trembled,

And some of the neighbours were so much afraid

That they started to ring up the Fire Brigade.

When suddenly, up from a small basement flat,

Why who should stalk out but the GREAT RUMPUSCAT.

His eyes were like fireballs fearfully blazing,

He gave a great yawn, and his jaws were amazing;

And when he looked out through the bars of the area,

You never saw anything fiercer or hairier.

And what with the glare of his eyes and his yawning,

The Pekes and the Pollicles quickly took warning.

He looked at the sky and he gave a great leap—

And they every last one of them scattered like sheep.


*And when the Police Dog returned to his beat,*

*There wasn't a single one left in the street.*

# 狮子狗与小破狗恶斗记

兼叙

哈巴狗和博美狗的参战

以及大闹猫加以干预

等若干事件


人人都知道，狮子狗和小破狗

傲慢而狂热，是不共戴天的死对头；

到处都一样，无论你往哪儿走。

还有哈巴狗和博美狗，尽管人们都讲

他们不喜欢打架，他们也会时常

出现渴望加入战团的一切症状。

然后他们

        汪汪汪汪

        汪汪**汪汪**

    直到你满公园都能听见他们叫嚷。


在我要讲述的故事开始之时

几乎已经有一个星期平安无事

（对小破狗和狮子狗来说可是好长时间）。

大块头警犬擅离自己的管片——

我不知道原因，但人们都认为

他溜进了砖瓦匠盾徽酒吧去喝一杯——

这时街上根本一个人影也没有，

狮子狗和小破狗好巧不巧碰了头。

他们不向前冲，也不完全退避，

他们怒目相视，用后脚刨地，

然后他们开始

　　　　汪汪汪汪

　　　　**汪汪汪汪**

　　直到你满公园都能听见他们叫嚷。


虽说人们讲话随心所欲，但狮子狗

不是英国狗，而是一只异邦的中国狗。

就这样，所有狮子狗都听到了骚动，

有的来到窗口，有的来到门洞；

肯定有一打，二十只也说不定。

他们一齐咕咕哝哝，呼哧呼哧，

用那叽里呱啦的中国话发泄怒气。

但是大吵大闹正是小破狗的喜好，

因为所谓小破狗就是约克郡土狗，犟头倔脑，

他的苏格兰表亲全是咬人的恶狗，

他们中间所有公狗都出名地好斗；

于是他们出了门，风笛手排列整齐，

奏起了《蓝帽苏格兰人越过边界之时》[1]。

这时哈巴狗和博美狗也不再置身事外，

有的来自屋顶，有的来自阳台，

加入到

这场喧嚣，

吠叫着

              汪汪汪汪

              汪汪**汪汪**

   直到你满公园都能听见他们叫嚷。


现在，当这帮胆大妄为的英豪聚首，

交通彻底瘫痪，地铁颤抖，

一些街坊邻居如此害怕，

他们开始给消防队打电话。

此刻突然从小小的地下公寓阔步踱出的，

---

[1] 《蓝帽苏格兰人越过边界之时》（*When the Blue Bonnets Came Over the Border*），苏格兰民歌。

除了**大闹猫**，还能是哪个？

他的眼睛好像火球，喷出骇人的烈焰，

他打了一个大哈欠，嘴巴令人惊叹。

当他透过地下室栅栏向外看去，

你绝没见过更凶残、更毛蓬蓬的东西。

他的怒视和哈欠里的信号，

让狮子狗和小破狗马上领受了警告。

他昂首向天，腾身跃起——

他们一个个都像小绵羊，四下散去。


当警犬又回到他的管片，

街上已经一只狗都不见。

# Mr.

# Mistoffelees

You ought to know Mr. Mistoffelees!

The Original Conjuring Cat—

(There can be no doubt about that).

Please listen to me and don't scoff. All his

Inventions are off his own bat.

There's no such Cat in the metropolis;

He holds all the patent monopolies

For performing surprising illusions

And creating eccentric confusions.

   At prestidigitation

      And at legerdemain

   He'll defy examination

      And deceive you again.

The greatest magicians have something to learn

From Mr. Mistoffelees' Conjuring Turn.

Presto!

   Away we go!

      And we all say: OH!

      Well I never!

      Was there ever

      A Cat so clever

         As Magical Mr. Mistoffelees!


He is quiet and small, he is black

From his ears to the tip of his tail;

He can creep through the tiniest crack,

He can walk on the narrowest rail.

He can pick any card from a pack,

He is equally cunning with dice;

He is always deceiving you into believing

That he's only hunting for mice.

He can play any trick with a cork

Or a spoon and a bit of fish-paste;

If you look for a knife or a fork

And you think it is merely misplaced—

You have seen it one moment, and then it is *gawn*!

But you'll find it next week lying out on the lawn.

And we all say: OH!

Well I never!

Was there ever

A Cat so clever

As Magical Mr. Mistoffelees!


His manner is vague and aloof,

You would think there was nobody shyer—

But his voice has been heard on the roof

When he was curled up by the fire.

And he's sometimes been heard by the fire

When he was about on the roof—

(At least we all *heard* somebody who purred)

Which is incontestable proof

Of his singular magical powers:

And I have known the family to call

Him in from the garden for hours,

While he was asleep in the hall.

And not long ago this phenomenal Cat

Produced *seven kittens* right out of a hat!

And we all said: OH!

Well I never!

Did you ever

Know a Cat so clever

As Magical Mr. Mistoffelees!

# 迷思托菲利斯先生

你应该知道迷思托菲利斯先生！

独创大师魔法猫——

（这是毋庸置疑的称号。）

请听我讲，不要发出嘲笑声。

他的创意全都出于自己的头脑。

这样的猫在大都会仅此一只；

他拥有全部的独家专利

来展示不可思议的幻觉

造成异乎寻常的惶惑。

　　会变戏法

　　　　也会上手段，

　　他会瞒过检查

　　　　再次把你蒙骗。

最伟大的魔术师也可以

从迷思托菲利斯先生的魔术节目中学到东西。

一二三!

变变变!

我们都说：噢!

我真没想到!

史上可曾

有猫如此聪明

一如魔术师迷思托菲利斯先生!


他安静而瘦小，浑身黑色

从耳朵一直到尾巴尖；

他能从最小的缝隙钻过，

他能走上最窄的横杆。

他能从一副牌里将任意一张抽取，

他同样会灵巧地掷骰子；

他总是哄得你确信无疑

他只不过是在捉耗子。

他能用软木塞变戏法，

也可以用勺子和一点鱼酱；

假如你去找一把餐刀或餐叉

　　以为它只是放错了地方——

你刚刚还看到它，转眼就不知去向！

可下星期你会发现，它就躺在外面草坪上。

　　我们都说：噢！

　　我真没想到！

　　史上可曾

　　有猫如此聪明

　　　　一如魔术师迷思托菲利斯先生！


他的态度暧昧而冷漠，

你会觉得没有猫比他更怕生——

可是当他在炉火旁蜷卧，

他的声音却听起来在屋顶。

有时他听着是在炉火前，

其实他正徘徊在屋顶——

（至少那咕噜声我们全都听见）

这就无可辩驳地证明

　　他拥有非凡的魔术法力：

　　　我还知道家人叫这只猫

　　从花园进屋，花了好几个小时，

其实他就在客厅睡大觉。

不久以前，这了不起的猫

又从一顶帽子里变出了七只小猫！

我们都说：噢！

我真没想到！

史上可曾

有猫如此聪明

一如魔术师迷思托菲利斯先生！

# Macavity:

## The

## Mystery Cat

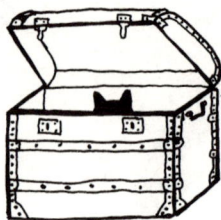

Macavity's a Mystery Cat: he's called the Hidden Paw—

For he's the master criminal who can defy the Law.

He's the bafflement of Scotland Yard, the Flying Squad's despair:

For when they reach the scene of crime—*Macavity's not there*!

Macavity, Macavity, there's no one like Macavity,

He's broken every human law, he breaks the law of gravity.

His powers of levitation would make a fakir stare,

And when you reach the scene of crime—*Macavity's not there*!

You may seek him in the basement, you may look up in the air—

But I tell you once and once again, *Macavity's not there*!

Macavity's a ginger cat, he's very tall and thin;

You would know him if you saw him, for his eyes are sunken in.

His brow is deeply lined with thought, his head is highly doomed;

His coat is dusty from neglect, his whiskers are uncombed.

He sways his head from side to side, with movements like a snake;

And when you think he's half asleep, he's always wide awake.

Macavity, Macavity, there's no one like Macavity,

For he's a fiend in feline shape, a monster of depravity.

You may meet him in a by-street, you may see him in the square—

But when a crime's discovered, then *Macavity's not there*!

He's outwardly respectable. (They say he cheats at cards.)

And his footprints are not found in any file of Scotland Yard's.

And when the larder's looted, or the jewel-case is rifled,

Or when the milk is missing, or another Peke's been stifled,

Or the greenhouse glass is broken, and the trellis past repair—

Ay, there's the wonder of the thing! *Macavity's not there*!

And when the Foreign Office finds a Treaty's gone astray,
Or the Admiralty lose some plans and drawings by the way,
There may be a scrap of paper in the hall or on the stair—
But it's useless of investigate—*Macavity's not there*!
And when the loss has been disclosed, the Secret Service say:
"It must have been Macavity!"—but he's a mile away.
You'll be sure to find him resting, or a-licking of his thumbs,
Or engaged in doing complicated long division sums.

Macavity, Macavity, there's no one like Macavity,
There never was a Cat of such deceitfulness and suavity.
He always has an alibi, and one or two to spare:
At whatever time the deed took place—MACAVITY WASN'T THERE!
And they say that all the Cats whose wicked deeds are widely known
(I might mention Mungojerrie, I might mention Griddlebone)
Are nothing more than agents for the Cat who all the time
Just controls their operations: the Napoleon of Crime!

# 麦卡维蒂：神秘猫

麦卡维蒂是一只神秘猫：江湖人称"迷踪爪"——

因为他是个犯罪大师，惯于违犯律条。

他让苏格兰场 [1] 困惑，令飞虎队 [2] 绝望：

因为他们到达罪案现场时——麦卡维蒂不在场！


麦卡维蒂，麦卡维蒂，独一无二的麦卡维蒂，

他破坏人类的所有法律，他打破万有引力定律。

他的腾空悬浮术会让一个托钵僧呆望，

你到达罪案现场时——麦卡维蒂不在场！

你可以去地下室找他，你可以抬头向空中张望——

但我再一次、再一次告诉你，麦卡维蒂不在场！


麦卡维蒂是一只橘猫，他又瘦又高；

你一见面就会认出他来，因为他的眼睛内凹。

他的额头深深刻满思想，他的脑袋是个浑圆球体；

他不修边幅，大衣满是灰尘，胡须从不梳理。

---

[1]  苏格兰场（Scotland Yard），英国伦敦警察厅的代称。

[2]  飞虎队（Flying Squad），即英国的快速特警队。

他把脑袋左摇右摆，动作就像一条蛇；

你以为他半梦半醒，其实他总是清醒的。


麦卡维蒂，麦卡维蒂，独一无二的麦卡维蒂，

因为他是一个猫形魔鬼，一个邪恶的怪东西。

你可能遇见他在小巷，你可能看见他在广场——

但罪案曝光之时，麦卡维蒂不在场！


他表面上正派得体。（他们说他打牌作弊。）

苏格兰场的任何档案里都找不到他的足迹。

当食品柜遭洗劫，或者首饰盒被顺走，

当牛奶失踪，或者又闷死了一只狮子狗，

或者温室玻璃被打碎，棚架修补无望——

唉，事情就是这么神奇！麦卡维蒂不在场！


当外交部发现有一份条约被盗去，

还有，海军部也遗失了一些计划和图纸，

可能会有一片碎纸在大厅里或楼梯上——

但是调查于事无补——麦卡维蒂不在场！

当遗失事件披露，情报局这样说道：

"一定是麦卡维蒂干的！"——但他远在一英里之遥。

你准会发现他在休息，或是舔手指，

或是专心做着复杂的长除法算术题。


麦卡维蒂，麦卡维蒂，独一无二的麦卡维蒂，

从没有一只猫这般奸诈又和气。

他总有不在场证明，以及一两个脱罪的伎俩：

无论恶行何时发生——**麦卡维蒂都不在场！**

他们说，所有那些罪行累累、恶名昭彰的猫

（我不妨提到呢绒夜壶，烤盘骨头也会提到）

都不过是在给这位猫王跑腿，他始终稳稳

控制着他们的行动：这犯罪界的拿破仑！

# Gus:

# The

# Theatre

# Cat

Gus is the Cat at the Theatre Door.

His name, as I ought to have told you before,

Is really Asparagus. That's such a fuss

To pronounce, that we usually call him just Gus.

His coat's very shabby, he's thin as a rake,

And he suffers from palsy that makes his paw shake.

Yet he was, in his youth, quite the smartest of Cats—

But no longer a terror to mice and to rats.

For he isn't the Cat that he was in his prime;

Though his name was quite famous, he says, in its time.

And whenever he joins his friends at their club

(Which takes place at the back of the neighbouring pub)

He loves to regale them, if someone else pays,

With anecdotes drawn from his palmiest days.

For he once was a Star of the highest degree—

He has acted with Irving, he's acted with Tree.

And he likes to relate his success on the Halls,

Where the Gallery once gave him seven cat-calls.

But his grandest creation, as he loves to tell,

Was Firefrorefiddle, the Fiend of the Fell.


"I have played," so he says, "every possible part,

And I used to know seventy speeches by heart.

I'd extemporize back-chat, I knew how to gag,

And I knew how to let the cat out of the bag.

I knew how to act with my back and my tail;

With an hour of rehearsal, I never could fail.

I'd a voice that would soften the hardest of hearts,

Whether I took the lead, or in character parts.

I have sat by the bedside of poor Little Nell;

When the Curfew was rung, then I swung on the bell.

In the Pantomime season I never fell flat,

And I once understudied Dick Whittington's Cat.

But my grandest creation, as history will tell,

Was Firefrorefiddle, the Fiend of the Fell."


Then, if someone will give him a toothful of gin,

He will tell how he once played a part in *East Lynne*.

At a Shakespeare performance he once walked on pat,

When some actor suggested the need for a cat.

He once played a Tiger—could do it again—

Which an Indian Colonel pursued down a drain.

And he thinks that he still can, much better than most,

Produce blood-curdling noises to bring on the Ghost.

And he once crossed the stage on a telegraph wire,

To rescue a child when a house was on fire.

And he says: "Now, these kittens,they do not get trained

As we did in the days when Victoria reigned.

They never get drilled in a regular troupe,

And they think they are smart, just to jump through a hoop."

And he'll say, as he scratches himself with his claws,

"Well, the Theatre's certainly not what it was.

These modern productions are all very well,

But there's nothing to equal, from what I hear tell,

That moment of mystery

When I made history

As Firefrorefiddle, the Fiend of the Fell."

# 嘎斯：剧院猫

嘎斯是剧院的看门猫。

他的大名，正如我曾跟你说到，

其实是阿斯帕拉嘎斯。这个讲究的名字

根本没法读，所以我们通常叫他嘎斯。

他衣衫褴褛，瘦得皮包骨头，

他患有痉挛症，那让他的爪子颤抖。

他年轻时可是一只绝顶聪明的猫——

但再也不能把大老鼠小耗子吓到。

因为他已不是全盛时期的那只猫；

不过当年他可是大名鼎鼎，他这样说道。

无论他何时去俱乐部会朋友

（地点就在隔壁酒馆的背后），

只要有人付账，他都喜欢用

当年风光时的奇闻异事给他们助兴。

因为他曾经是个明星，跻身顶级——

他和欧文 [1] 同过台，他跟特里 [2] 搭过戏。

---

[1] 欧文（Sir Henry Irving，1838—1905），英国著名戏剧演员兼经纪人。

[2] 特里（Sir Herbert Beerbohm Tree，1852—1917），英国著名戏剧演员。

他喜欢把自己在音乐厅的成功摆一摆，

有一次，顶层楼座的观众向他喝了七次倒彩。

但是正如他所津津乐道，他塑造的最佳角色

是冰火混混，丘陵地带的恶魔。


"我扮演过各类角色，"他这样说，

"七十段台词我都背出过。

我能即席表演抬杠，我知道如何搞笑，

我也知道如何故意露马脚。

我知道如何用后背和尾巴加戏，

排练上个把小时，就绝对不会出岔子。

我的声音能让最硬的心柔软，

无论是挑大梁，还是以配角出演。

我曾坐在可怜的小耐儿[1]病榻旁；

当宵禁钟声响起，我在钟上悠荡。

在圣诞童话剧演出季，我从未失败过，

---

[1] 小耐儿，查尔斯·狄更斯小说《老古玩店》中的角色。

我曾经出演狄克·惠廷顿[1]之猫的B角。

但是历史会证明，我塑造的最佳角色

是冰火混混，丘陵地带的恶魔。"


于是，如果有人愿意给他一口琴酒喝，

他就会大讲如何在《魂断东林》[2]中扮演角色。

有一次演莎剧，他走起路来啪啪响，

因为有个演员建议把一只猫加上。

他演过一只老虎——再演一次也无妨——

被一个印度上校在下水道里紧追不放。

他觉得他比大多数猫都强，还能

发出恐怖的怪叫，招来幽灵。

他还曾踩着一根电话线穿过舞台，

去失火的房子里救一个小孩。

他说："现如今，这些小猫咪啊，他们训练不够，

不比我们当年，维多利亚女王在位的时候。

他们从没在正规剧团练过功，

自以为挺聪明，只知道唯命是从。"

---

[1] 狄克·惠廷顿（Dick Whittington，1350—1423），英国商人，曾三次担任伦敦市长。在传说中，惠廷顿的猫帮助他发家致富。

[2] 《魂断东林》（*East Lynne*），英国女作家艾伦·伍德的小说。

他还会一边用爪子抓痒，一边说：

"唉，剧院已经完全不是原来的样子了。

这些摩登的演出的确都很棒，

可是就我所见，怎么都比不上

　　我创造历史的

　　神秘时刻

出演冰火混混，丘陵地带的恶魔。"

# Bustopher Jones:

# The Cat

# about Town

Bustopher Jones is *not* skin and bones—

In fact, he's remarkably fat.

He doesn't haunt pubs—he has eight or nine clubs,

For he's the St. James's Street Cat!

He's the Cat we all greet as he walks down the street

In his coat of fastidious black:

No commonplace mousers have such well-cut trousers

Or such an impreccable back.

In the whole of St. James's the smartest of names is

The name of this Brummell of Cats;

And we're all of us proud to be nodded or bowed to

By Bustopher Jones in white spats!


His visits are occasional to the *Senior Educational*

And it is against the rules

For any one Cat to belong both to that

And the *Joint Superior Schools.*

For a similar reason, when game is in season

He is found, not at *Fox's,* but *Blimp's;*

He is frequently seen at the gay *Stage and Screen*

Which is famous for winkles and shrimps.

In the season of venison he gives his ben'son

To the *Pothunter's* succulent bones;

And just before noon's not a moment too soon

To drop in for a drink at the *Drones.*

When he's seen in a hurry there's probably curry

At the *Siamese*—or at the *Glutton;*

If he looks full of gloom then he's lunched at the *Tomb*

On cabbage, rice pudding and mutton.

So, much in this way, passes Bustopher's day—

At one club or another he's found.

It can cause no surprise that under our eyes

He has grown unmistakably round.

He's a twenty-five pounder, or I am a bounder,

And he's putting on weight every day:

But he's so well preserved because he's observed

All his life a routine, so he'll say.

And (to put it in rhyme) "I shall last out my time"

Is the word for this stoutest of Cats.

It must and it shall be Spring in Pall Mall

While Bustopher Jones wears white spats!

# 巴士托弗·琼斯：城市游荡猫

巴士托弗·琼斯并不瘦得皮包骨——

实际上，他胖得出人意料。

他不泡酒吧——他加入了俱乐部八九家，

因为他是圣詹姆士街的猫！

当他穿着一丝不苟，身披黑大衣走上街头，

我们都要向这位名猫致意：

普通捕鼠猫可穿不起这样剪裁得当的裤子，

后背也不是这样无可挑剔。

在整个圣詹姆士，最气派的名字就是

这位猫中布鲁梅尔[1]的名号；

当巴士托弗·琼斯穿着白鞋罩对我们点头哈腰

我们全都引以为傲！


他偶尔会去造访耆英教育

而这违反了律条，

任何一只猫都不可以既属于那里

---

[1] 布鲁梅尔（George Bryan "Beau" Brummell，1778—1840），英国摄政时期的时尚权威。

也属于联合高等学校。

出于同样的道理，当野味正好应季，

他没去狐狸屋，却去了老顽固之家；

他频繁进出乐趣多多的舞台银幕，

那里最有名的是玉黍螺和虾。

在鹿肉当令的时候，他把祝福全都

给了火锅猎手多汁的肉骨头；

趁着时间刚好，正午时分还没到，

他顺路去雄蜂喝上一口。

如果见他匆匆忙忙，那可能是咖喱香

飘出了暹罗人——或者饕餮兽；

如果他脸色暗淡，那就是在土墓用了午餐，

吃的是圆白菜、大米布丁和羊肉。


所以，就用这种方式，巴士托弗打发着日子——

在这家或那家俱乐部现身。

没什么好惊讶，就在我们眼皮底下

他明显变得圆滚滚。

他有二十五磅沉，我要瞎说就不是人，

而他的体重每天都在增长：

不过他保养得真好，因为大家注意到

如他所言，他一生起居有常。

他还说（化成了诗句）"我将坚持到底"，

此话就出自这只肥猫。

蓓尔美尔街理所当然会迎来春天

当巴士托弗·琼斯穿上白鞋罩！

# Skimbleshanks:

# The

# Railway Cat

There's a whisper down the line at 11.39

When the Night Mail's ready to depart,

Saying "Skimble where is Skimble has he gone to hunt the thimble?

We must find him or the train can't start."

All the guards and all the porters and the stationmaster's daughters

They are searching high and low,

Saying "Skimble where is Skimble for unless he's very nimble

Then the Night Mail just can't go."

At 11.42 then the signal's nearly due

And the passengers are frantic to a man—

Then Skimble will appear and he'll saunter to the rear:

He's been busy in the luggage van!

    He gives one flash of his glass-green eyes

        And the signal goes "All Clear!"

    And we're off at last for the northern part

        Of the Northern Hemisphere!


You may say that by and large it is Skimble who's in charge

Of the Sleeping Car Express.

From the driver and the guards to the bagmen playing cards

He will supervise them all, more or less.

Down the corridor he paces and examines all the faces

Of the travellers in the First and the Third;

He establishes control by a regular patrol

And he'd know at once if anything occurred.

He will watch you without winking and he sees what you are thinking

And it's certain that he doesn't approve

Of hilarity and riot, so the folk are very quiet

When Skimble is about and on the move.

You can play no pranks with Skimbleshanks!

He's a Cat that cannot be ignored;

So nothing goes wrong on the Northern Mail

When Skimbleshanks is aboard.


Oh it's very pleasant when you have found your little den

With your name written up on the door.

And the berth is very neat with a newly folded sheet

And there's not a speck of dust on the floor.

There is every sort of light—you can make it dark or bright;

There's a button that you turn to make a breeze.

There's a funny little basin you're supposed to wash your face in

And a crank to shut the window if you sneeze.

Then the guard looks in politely and will ask you very brightly

"Do you like your morning tea weak or strong?"

But Skimble's just behind him and was ready to remind him,

For Skimble won't let anything go wrong.

And when you creep into your cosy berth

And pull up the counterpane,

You are bound to admit that it's very nice

To know that you won't be bothered by mice—

You can leave all that to the Railway Cat,

The Cat of the Railway Train!


In the middle of the night he is always fresh and bright;

Every now and then he has a cup of tea

With perhaps a drop of Scotch while he's keeping on the watch,

Only stopping here and there to catch a flea.

You were fast asleep at Crewe and so you never knew

That he was walking up and down the station;

You were sleeping all the while he was busy at Carlisle,

Where he greets the stationmaster with elation.

But you saw him at Dumfries, where he summons the police

If there's anything they ought to know about:

When you get to Gallowgate there you do not have to wait—

For Skimbleshanks will help you to get out!

 He gives you a wave of his long brown tail

  Which says: "I'll see you again!

 You'll meet without fail on the Midnight Mail

  The Cat of the Railway Train."

# 废话脚杆：铁路猫

时间是 11 点 39 分，传来窃窃私语一阵，

在夜班邮车准备出发的时刻

嘀咕着，"废话呢废话去哪儿了，难道是去追顶针了？

我们必须找到他，否则就发不了车。"

所有列车员和搬运工人，还有站长家的千金们，

他们忙着四下里搜查，

嘀咕着，"废话呢废话去哪儿了？除非他动作够敏捷，

否则夜班邮车就不能出发。"

11 点 42 分，信号灯显示发车将近，

旅客们朝着一个人发泄愤怒——

这时废话会露头，一派悠闲向车尾走：

原来他一直在行李车里忙碌！

　　他那草绿色的眼睛闪了一闪，

　　　　信号灯显示："警报解除！"

　　我们终于得以上路，驶向

　　　　北半球的北部！

你看，总的来说，是废话在全权负责

这班卧铺特快列车。

从司机和列车员到玩纸牌的小贩，

差不多都在他管理之列。

他沿着过道溜达，仔细检查

头等车和三等车所有旅客的面孔；

他的巡逻很有规律，建立了控制体系；

他马上就会知道有什么事情发生。

他会不错眼珠盯着你，看透你的心思，

他理所当然不赞成

欢笑和骚动，所以人们非常安静

假如废话就在附近走动。

　　你可不能跟废话脚杆耍花招！

　　　　他是一只不容忽视的猫；

　　所以有了废话脚杆在车上

　　　　北方邮车什么事都不会弄糟。


当你发现你的小包厢有你名字写在门上，

哦，这可真是暖心。

铺位非常整洁，床单新叠过，

地板上没有一粒灰尘。

车上的灯各式各样——你可以调暗或调亮；

按下按钮可以带给你清风一缕。

有个小洗手盆很好玩，你就用它来洗脸，

摇曲柄可以关车窗，要是你打喷嚏。

列车员礼貌地探进头，乖巧地向你问候：

"您的早茶是要淡一些还是浓一些？"

但是他后面就跟着废话，时刻准备提醒他，

因为废话不允许出任何差错。

　　当你爬进舒适的铺位

　　　　把床单掀掉，

　　你必须承认这有多美妙，

　　你知道不会受到老鼠困扰——

　　你可以把这些烂事全甩给铁路猫，

　　　　列车上的铁路猫！


一到了半夜里，他就总是充满活力；

他有时会喝杯茶，

也许加一滴威士忌，这让能他保持警惕，

只是抓跳蚤才会偶尔停下。

到克鲁时你睡得正熟，所以根本不清楚

他正在车站走来走去；

到卡莱尔你昏睡不醒，他却忙个不停，

兴高采烈地向站长致意。

不过你在邓弗里斯看见了他，他正召集警察训话，

发生任何事他们都该知道怎么办：

当你抵达加洛盖特，你没必要干等着——

因为废话脚杆会帮你出站！

　　他将棕色的长尾巴朝你一扬，

　　　　意思是："下次再见！

　　你肯定将在午夜邮车上

　　　　与列车上的铁路猫相见。"

# The
# Ad-dressing
# of Cats

You've read of several kinds of Cat,
And my opinion now is that
You should need no interpreter
To understand their character.
You now have learned enough to see
That Cats are much like you and me
And other people whom we find
Possessed of various types of mind.
For some are sane and some are mad
And some are good and some are bad
And some are better, some are worse—
But all may be described in verse.
You've seen them both at work and games,
And learnt about their proper names,
Their habits and their habitat:
But

*How would you ad-dress a Cat?*

So first, your memory I'll jog,

And say: A CAT IS NOT A DOG.


Now Dogs pretend they like to fight;

They often bark, more seldom bite;

But yet a Dog is, on the whole,

What you would call a simple soul.

Of course I'm not including Pekes,

And such fantastic canine freaks.

The usual Dog about the Town

Is much inclined to play the clown,

And far from showing too much pride

Is frequently undignified.

He's very easily taken in—

Just chuck him underneath the chin

Or slap his back or shake his paw,

And he will gambol and guffaw.

He's such an easy-going lout,

He'll answer any hail or shout.

Again I must remind you that
A Dog's a Dog—A CAT'S A CAT.

With Cats, some say, one rule is true:
*Don't speak till you are spoken to.*
Myself, I do not hold with that—
I say, you should ad-dress a Cat.
But always keep in mind that he
Resents familiarity.
I bow, and taking off my hat,
Ad-dress him in this form: O CAT!
But if he is the Cat next door,
Whom I have often met before
(He comes to see me in my flat)
I greet him with an OOPSA CAT!
I've heard them call him James Buz-James—
But we've not got so far as names.
Before a Cat will condescend
To treat you as a trusted friend,
Some little token of esteem
Is needed, like a dish of cream;
And you might now and then supply
Some caviare, or Strassburg Pie,
Some potted grouse, or salmon paste—
He's sure to have his personal taste.
(I know a Cat, who makes a habit
Of eating nothing else but rabbit,

And when he's finished, licks his paws

So's not to waste the onion sauce.)

A Cat's entitled to expect

These evidences of respect.

And so in time you reach your aim,

And finally call him by his NAME.


So this is this, and that is that:

And there's how you AD-DRESS A CAT.

# 猫的称呼

你已经读到了好多种猫，

现在来听听我的忠告，

你应该不需要解说者

就能理解他们的性格。

你现在已经学得够多，

会发现猫儿就像你我，

也像我们认识的其他人，

有着不同类型的心神。

有的理智，有的疯癫，

有的是好猫，有的是坏蛋，

有的更好，有的更坏——

但都可以用诗描述出来。

你见过他们工作和游戏，

学过关于他们的专有名词，

知道他们的习惯和窝巢：

可是

　　　你打算怎样称呼一只猫？

所以首先，我要请你记在心头，

一句话：**猫不是狗**。


话说狗们假装喜欢争斗打闹；

他们常常吠叫，却很少真咬；

不过总的来说，你可以称呼

一只狗为头脑简单的动物。

当然我把狮子狗排除在外，

他们都是诡异的犬科怪胎。

在城里游荡的寻常狗

特别喜欢出乖弄丑，

远谈不上有多么傲慢，

倒一再表现得丢人现眼。

他很容易上当变节——

只须摸一摸他的下巴颏，

在他后背拍拍，把他爪子摇摇，

他就会欢跳、傻笑。

他就是这么个随和的呆瓜，

任谁招呼他他都答话。


我必须再次请你记牢，

狗是狗——**猫是猫**。


说起猫，据说有个不易之法：

猫不跟你说话，你就别招他。

我自己嘛，我可不管那一套——

要我说，你得会称呼猫。

不过一定要牢牢记住

他最讨厌套近乎。

我会鞠躬，脱帽，

这样称呼他：**喔，猫！**

不过假如是隔壁的猫，

我以前经常见到

（是他往我的公寓跑），

我会这样向他问候：**哎哟喂，猫！**

我听过他们叫他詹姆斯·巴兹－詹姆斯——

但我们还没熟到互称名字。

如果想让一只猫纡尊降贵

把你当作可靠的朋友坦诚以对，

总应该有所表示，

比如一碟奶油，略致敬意；

你可以时不常地供奉

一些鱼子酱，或是斯特拉斯堡小馅饼[1]，

一些鲑鱼糜，或是松鸡罐头——

他肯定有自己喜好的一口。

（我认识一只猫，他有个习惯，

只吃兔肉，别的一星儿都不沾，

吃完以后还要舔爪子，

以免浪费了洋葱汁。）

一只猫有资格期待你

拿出这些表示尊重的证据。

这样，有一天你会达到目的，

最终用他的**名字**跟他称兄道弟。


所以情况就是这样了：

这就是如何**称呼一只猫**的秘诀。


_____

[1] 斯特拉斯堡小馅饼（Strassburg Pie），一种鹅肝泥馅的法式点心。

THE AD-DRESSING
OF
CATS

# Cat

# Morgan

# Introduces

# Himself

I once was a Pirate what sailed the 'igh seas—
    But now I've retired as a com-mission-aire:
And that's how you find me a-takin' my ease
    And keepin' the door in a Bloomsbury Square.

I'm partial to partridges, likewise to grouse,
    And I favour that Devonshire cream in a bowl;
But I'm allus content with a drink on the 'ouse
    And a bit o' cold fish when I done me patrol.

I ain't got much polish, me manners is gruff,
    But I've got a good coat, and I keep meself smart;
And everyone says, and I guess that's enough:
    "You can't but like Morgan, 'e's got a kind 'art."

I got knocked about on the Barbary Coast,
    And me voice it ain't no sich melliferous horgan;
But yet I can state, and I'm not one to boast,
    That some of the gals is dead keen on old Morgan.

So if you'ave business with Faber—or Faber—
    I'll give you this tip, and it's worth a lot more:
You'll save yourself time, and you'll spare yourself labour
    If jist you make friends with the Cat at the door.

MORGAN

# 摩根猫自我介绍

我原先是个海盗，在公海上航行——

　　但现在已经洗手不干，当了个看门人；

就这么着你瞧见我一身轻松

　　在布鲁姆斯伯里一个广场看门。


我爱吃山鹬，也爱吃松鸡，

　　我喜欢德文郡奶油盛在碗里；

不过能免费喝一杯我就满意，

　　最好巡逻完了还能来点冷鱼。


我没啥教养，脾气也挺臭，

　　可我有件好衣裳，让我自个儿挺光鲜；

人人都这么说，我觉着那就足够：

　　"你没法不喜欢摩根，他这伙计好心眼。"


我在柏柏里海岸 [1] 挨过揍，

---

[1]　柏柏里海岸（Barbary Coast），北非地中海沿岸地区，范围从埃及延伸至大西洋。

我的嗓音也不像管风琴那么甜；

不过我倒敢说，咱可不是吹牛，

　　有几个妞儿对老摩根特别稀罕。


所以你要是有业务找费伯——或者费伯公司 [1]——

　　我会给你支个着儿，这可值老钱喽：

你能节省时间，还能节省力气，

　　只要你肯跟看门猫交朋友。


**摩根**

---

[1] 费伯公司（Faber），即艾略特当时工作的费伯出版公司（Faber & Faber）。

**图书在版编目（CIP）数据**

老负鼠的现世猫书 ：汉英对照／（英）T.S.艾略特
著；雷格译；姜瑾绘 . —— 北京 ：国际文化出版公司，
2020.11

ISBN 978-7-5125-1231-3

I. ①老… II. ①T… ②雷… ③姜… III. ①英语－
汉语－对照读物 ②儿童诗歌－诗集－英国－现代 IV.
① H319.4；I

中国版本图书馆 CIP 数据核字（2020）第 153887 号

**老负鼠的现世猫书**

| | | |
|---|---|---|
| 作　　者 | ［英］T.S.艾略特 | |
| 译　　者 | 雷　格 | |
| 绘　　者 | 姜　瑾 | |
| 责任编辑 | 宋亚晅 | |
| 特约编辑 | 卢倩倩 | |
| 统筹监制 | 文　钊 | |
| 策划编辑 | 邓锦辉　文　雯 | |
| 封面设计 | 今亮后声 HOPESOUND pankouyugu@163.com | |
| 出版发行 | 国际文化出版公司 | |
| 经　　销 | 全国新华书店 | |
| 印　　刷 | 山东临沂新华印刷物流集团有限责任公司 | |
| 开　　本 | 710 毫米 ×1000 毫米　16 开 | |
| | 10 印张　　　　　　100 千字 | |
| 版　　次 | 2020 年 11 月第 1 版 | |
| | 2020 年 11 月第 1 次印刷 | |
| 书　　号 | ISBN 978-7-5125-1231-3 | |
| 定　　价 | 68.00 元 | |

国际文化出版公司
北京朝阳区东土城路乙 9 号　　邮编：100013
总编室：（010）64270995　　传真：（010）64271578
销售热线：（010）64271187
传真：（010）64271187—800
E-mail：icpc@95777.sina.net